I0154169

Hugh Miller Thompson

**The world and the Logos**

Hugh Miller Thompson

**The world and the Logos**

ISBN/EAN: 9783337817954

Hergestellt in Europa, USA, Kanada, Australien, Japan

Cover: Foto ©ninafisch / pixelio.de

Weitere Bücher finden Sie auf **www.hansebooks.com**

# THE

# WORLD AND THE LOGOS

BY

HUGH MILLER THOMPSON, S.T.D., LL.D.

*Assistant Bishop of Mississippi*

NEW YORK & LONDON

G. P. PUTNAM'S SONS

The Knickerbocker Press

1886

# EXTRACTS

From the communication of the donors to the Board of Trustees of the Theological Seminary of the Diocese of Ohio and Kenyon College.

CLEVELAND, June 21, 1880.

GENTLEMEN:

We have consecrated and set apart for the service of God the sum of $5,000, to be devoted to the establishment of a lecture or lectures in the Institutions at Gambier on the Evidences of Natural and Revealed Religion; or the Relations of Science and Religion.

We ask permission of the Trustees to establish the lecture immediately, with the following provisions:

The lecture or lectures shall be delivered biennially on Founders' Day (if such a day shall be established), or other appropriate time. During our lifetime, or the lifetime of either of us, the nomination of the lectureship shall rest with us.

The interest for two years on the fund, less the sum necessary to pay for the publication, shall be paid to the Lecturer.

The Lecturer shall also have one half of the net profits of the publication during the first two years after the date of publication. All other profits shall be the property of the Board, and shall be added to the capital of the lectureship.

We express our preference that the lecture or lectures shall be delivered in the Church of the Holy Spirit, if such building be in existence; and shall be delivered in the presence of all the members of the Institutions under the authority of the Board.

We ask that the day on which the lecture or the first of each series of lectures shall be delivered, shall be declared a holiday.

We wish that the nomination to this lectureship shall be restricted by no other consideration than the ability of the appointee to discharge the duty to the highest glory of God in the completest presentation of the subject. We desire that the lectures shall be published in uniform shape, and that a copy of each shall be placed in the libraries of Bexley Hall, Kenyon College and of the Philomethesian and the Nu Pi Kappa Society. Asking the favorable consideration of the Board of Trustees,

We remain with great respect,

G. T. BEDELL,
JULIA BEDELL.

The Board accepted the gift, approved the terms, named All Saints' Day, November the first, as Founders' Day, and made it a holiday.

# LECTURE FIRST.

"IN THE BEGINNING WAS THE WORD."

St. John's Gospel, i., 1.

THE New Testament, like the Old, begins with beginnings. Both, also, begin with *Reason.*[1] Each introduces us into an ordered universe—a kosmos, forming or formed out of a chaos. In each, also, this kosmos is crowned, as by the highest creative activity of the Eternal Logos, by a rational being, a finite Logos, breathed out from the Infinite One, and made in the image and the likeness of that.

And for this finite Logos all the kosmos exists. He is, in a sense, its lord, the viceroy over it, and has it in charge to render it more

---

[1] Whatever we may conclude with regard to the Mosaic account of creation, so-called, this is to be said for it : that it is plain, coherent, logical in itself, accounting for all the facts,—and that, so far, it is the only cosmogony of which this can be said.

The mythical cosmogonies of India or Scandinavia, with their supporting Tortoises or Life-Trees, are clearly poetical escapes from difficulties. The doctrine of evolution, so-called, does not deal with the question of creation at all—dodges, that is, all the difficulties.

I

orderly, more cosmical, more rational during its continuance.

There are voices called scientific, which deny all this and more. How profoundly contradictory to the utterance of St. John in the fourth gospel, these voices are, few have perhaps considered. That science is opposed in some way to the first chapter of Genesis, is more or less clear in the minds of intelligent believers. But that it is, in its latest reaches, opposed quite as irreconcilably, and on profounder philosophy, to the Gospel of St. John, is not so commonly understood.

For in this first chapter there is a method of creation stated, and a philosophy of creation as well.

The philosophy is this: Eternal Reason existed antecedent to all else. This Eternal Reason was with God, was God, and created all things. In this Reason was life, independent existence, and light, all illumination material and immaterial, and the Eternal Reason made a reasonable, rational world, a kosmos.

The purpose of this making was so definite, had so clear an end and meaning, that to carry it out fully when due time came, the Eternal Reason put Himself under the conditions of

humanity, which He had made in His own
image : " The Word became flesh and tented [2]
among us."

Now the latest voices of science join issue
with all this. They declare that there are no
beginnings, that beginnings are "unthinkable."
They tell us that nothing was made, that all
things have just grown. They insist that
there was no reason in the making, and that
there is no reason in the continuance, that
there is no purpose anywhere, no end for
which any thing exists, and that a purposeless
world glimmers upon its little road for a few
years, more or less, with its little population
of insects and fishes, birds and reptiles, worms
and men, till it swings back into the fire-mist
and weltering chaos out of which it was once
shot, red-hot, by some accident, some where,
and at some time, of which when and where
we are and must be entirely ignorant. [3]

---

[2] ἐσκήνωσεν.

[3] Evolution necessarily begins with something already existing. It
leaves the question of creation and its purposes untouched as insolu-
ble. In the philosophy of Mr. Spencer, matter is self-existent, and
the universe, or parts of it, vibrate forth from the fire-mist of the
supposed nebulæ into plants, animals, men, governments, religions,
and philosophies, and then back into fire-mist again. Mr. S. says :
"The absolute commencement (Anglicé, beginning) of organic life on
the globe I distinctly deny. The affirmation of universal evolution is,
in itself, the negative of an absolute commencement of any thing."

Between these two conceptions of the world's
cause and meaning no reconciliation is possible.    I want you to understand this at the
threshold.

There is a vague idea that "science," as it is
called, is opposed to religion, that it has en-
dangered our faith, and that religion needs to
be reconciled with it.    There is a notion common, too, that the reconciliation is possible,
that we only need to find some new explanation for some chapters in Genesis, make some
trifling changes of readings in our Bibles, and
a reconciliation between science and religion
will follow.

To effect this desirable end many simple-
minded and honest men are at work on both
sides, with various results.

But let us understand at the beginning, that
what arrogates for itself to-day the name of
science as its special own—the theory of evolution, namely, and, in biology, the theory of
descent—prides itself on a denial of any beginnings, a denial of any rational continuance or
intelligent purpose, a denial of any making,
and a denial of any intended end.

It is not a dealing with the Mosaic account
of the creation.    It is a theory which denies all

creation and compels you to assert that there
is not, and never was, a Logos at all, and that
Jesus Christ was, like all other men as well as
all organized things, an outcome of Bathybi-
an slime! Across the iron working of me-
chanic fatalism can come no reason, either of
God or men, either finite or infinite. One act
of self-centred will, one stroke of resolute self-
organizing purpose would annihilate the entire
philosophy of evolution, as the discovery of a
star whose motion is upon right angles, would
destroy the Newtonian theory.

That science and revealed religion are not
antagonistic, we are fond here of believing.
That seeming contentions can be reconciled,
we feel certain. But let us understand what
we say. Here, as in so many cases, we need
definitions.

If by science we mean theories based, not
on demonstration, but on assumptions made *a
priori*, on inferences, not from facts, but from
words and formulas ; if, in short, we allow a
metaphysics to be imposed upon us as natural
science, we shall find the reconciliation impossible, and useless, if it were not impossible.

Let us define science. If we understand by
science ordered human knowledge, we shall
not be far wrong.

In science, therefore, are two things : the facts, and the ordering of the facts.

There is a possibility of error about both.

1. The fact may not be truly ascertained.

2. The inference drawn from the fact, the meaning we find in it, the story it tells us, may be mistaken.[a]

The collector of facts exercises one set of human faculties. The organizer of the facts into their place in a logical science, exercises quite another and a higher. The first needs, mainly, quick, correct perceptions. The other requires a trained, logical intellect.

Farther still. The fact-collector may be of the highest excellence in his department, and

---

a Sir Charles Lyell ("Antiquity of Man") has some discussions upon a human pelvic bone, found in Mississippi mud near Natchez, and on a human skeleton found in the same mud near New Orleans, *sixteen feet* below the surface. Dr. Dowling, a New Orleans physician of some note, assigned to this skeleton, from calculations of the mud deposit of the Delta, an antiquity of 50,000 years ; other geologists give it 100,000.

Sir Charles gives 100,000 years to the formation of the Delta, from a calculation of the annual mud deposit.

During this autumn (1885) while sinking an artesian well for a "Cold Storage Warehouse" in New Orleans, the head of a *child's china doll* was brought up from a depth of *twenty-five* feet below the surface of the most solid ground, on which heavy buildings stand in the city of New Orleans (*New Orleans' Picayune*, Sept. 18, 1885). What has been said of medicine may be said of other sciences, especially geology. "There is nothing so uncertain as scientific *theories*, except scientific *facts*."

quite useless in the logical dealing with his discoveries. And the intellect best trained and fitted to see the meaning, bearing, and classification of facts may really never have discovered one !

There can be, in true science, also, no authorities. Names in science have no weight. The facts themselves are sacred. Being genuine facts, no denial, no ignorance, no sophistry touches them. But the uses made of them in any theory, the conclusions drawn from them, and the place, in any system, assigned them, are always subject to revision ; because, while the fact itself is infallible, the reasoning about it is always fallible, and often, as the event has shown, very fallible and blundering indeed.[4]

In the widest sense we are compelled to say that, the facts set aside, science has in it that element of human fallibility which makes it quite impossible to assert that any of its conclusions may not require re-examination.

---

[4] The history of the various editions of Sir Charles Lyell's "Principles of Geology" is a striking illustration. The amiable naturalist with precisely the same facts before him, through eight editions taught the permanency of species and the doctrine of specific creation. In the tenth, without a solitary new fact, he proclaims his adherence to the theory of evolution. The change was subjective, and accidentally shows a man's responsibility for his faith—how entirely his scientific faith even is of his own making.

It is no presumption, on the part of any thinking man, to take the sceptical position with regard to even the best-established conclusion of science, and call upon it again to give a reason for its existence.

We understand, of course, that, in the larger definition of science, theories must come in, working hypotheses, which are understood to be tentative, although assumed for the time as certain. But how effectual a theory may be as working hypothesis, and how absurdly false in fact, is shown in this, that the Ptolemaic theory served for ages for the working of all problems in practical astronomy. But a " working hypothesis " is not a part of science, though it may explain many things, and help in the discovery of genuine fact.

From what I have said, you will perceive that I decline to be overawed by names in science, and I decline also to accept conclusions, derived from facts, the validity of which depends upon the correctness of human reason, as being necessarily infallible or not amenable to my own re-examination, and to be accepted or rejected by my own judgment.

And just here all of us have the right, and I believe it is our duty, to protest respectfully but firmly against the tone assumed by some scientific men. That tone is thoroughly unscientific, dogmatic, and intolerant. There is, for instance, no measure to the contempt and scorn which such a writer as the German Oscar Schmidt treats those who hold to the doctrine of design, who claim to see any purpose or meaning in any thing whatever in the universe.[5]

Such a temper unfits a man for scientific discussion, and its manifestation puts him outside the bounds of that comity which is the law between thinking and serious men.

And yet, though this writer is peculiarly offensive, he only goes a little beyond what is the common attitude of many " scientific " men, so-called, towards believers in God, and especially believers in revelation. Dogmatism, intolerance of contradiction, assertion to be taken without reasoning, sneers at religion and religious ideas as blindness, childishness, and superstition, the assumption that a Christian believer cannot understand science, and is ruled out of scientific discussion,—all this is illustrated in the writings of men of a certain school, too commonly to need citations here in

---

[5] " The Doctrine of Descent, and Darwinism," by Oscar Schmidt.

proof, and this, in the face of that bede-roll of splendid names which have adorned science and religion equally.

We owe it to ourselves to resent this un-scientific and even insulting attitude.

No attainments in science make a man in-fallible.  No name, in that field at least, is sacred.  No work done within it but lies open to the cold irreverent criticism, and the passion-less judgment, of any man who insists on doing his own thinking and is competent to the doing it.

Because " I believe in God the Father Al-mighty, Maker of heaven and earth, and of all things visible and invisible," I shall not allow myself to be warned off the study of that Fath-er's works and worlds, because some modern scientist has concluded, since he finds not that Maker in his crucible nor under his microscope, that therefore there is no Maker at all, or, if there be, that, as Mr. Spencer majestically in-forms me, nobody can know any thing about Him.

One is tempted to put together just here the names of the scientific thinkers, beginning with Bacon, who have been and are Christians, and the names of those who hold that the world has no maker, and ask the latter if they rule Bacon and Newton out.

One, at all events, can well afford to sit in their unscientific and superstitious company. But I have set myself to call no man Rabbi here, and to bring no authority from a name.

There is nothing in the history of science, considering its theories and hypotheses as a part of science, which entitles it to stand upon the certainty of any theory of to-day.

When one considers the theories that have perished in chemistry, until the new chemistry, with the hypothesis of unitary structure, has seated itself amid the ruins of the old; in geology, from the theories of the Plutonists and Neptunists to the evolutionary,—a man like Sir Charles Lyell going through them all in his own lifetime, and the successive editions of one book; in biology, the corpuscular, the fluid, the chemical theories, and now the contending material and psychical; the emission and undulatory theories of light, the vortices of Descartes, and the attraction of Newton; the Ptolemaic "cycles and epicycles, orb in orb," and the Copernican central sun in astronomy; the phlogistic, caloric, and molecular theories of heat; in view, in short, of explanatory

theories painfully wrought out, painfully defended, universally accepted as sufficient, and
universally exploded at last, he is a very rash
man who will dare to assert that any existing
theory is a finality, and a very irrational and
impertinent man who, assuming its infallibility,
will insist that I must deny the existence of
God, because his personal scientific theory
does not need a God !

But if one goes behind the theory, be it
what it may, to the very facts on which the
theory is supposed to be founded, he finds
himself in a mist of uncertainty.  This Pro-
teus matter, with which natural science deals,
and which alone, some wise men say, is worth
our study, is not to be measured, weighed,
seen, nor bounded.  It forever eludes us.  We
have no instruments to gauge it.  There is no
absolute measure or weight in nature.  There
is a variable in all our calculations.  Never
yet had we an exact pound, an exact foot, or
yard ; and no man, with most perfect instruments, ever drew an exact circle, or an exact
square.  Kepler's laws are ideal, not actual.
Newton's calculations are true in the heavens
of the intellect, and not in the heavens of our
stars.  There is no perfect ellipse, no exact

orbit, no equal movements among the stars in their courses.

On matter everywhere, and all its doings, is the stamp of uncertainty, and an allowance for error must come into every experiment, and be admitted in our best tested. and most assured fact. No man knows, better than the scientific man, the element of error which underlies our most careful and conscientious dealing with matter. It plays us tricks continually, and at last modern science, in despair of it, has relegated it, under the name of atom, (if it really admit of existence at all), into the infinite dark of blank agnosticism, where no sense can test it, no microscope detect it, but where, at all events, it has the certainty of an ideal.

For, as a matter of fact, when it comes to the last issue, the only real things, the only true and abiding things, the only measurable and weighable things, are things ideal.

The mathematical line of Euclid is straight. No line drawn by man ever was. Euclid's point existed and forever exists, but only in the thought of the thinker. The line, the point, the angle are abiding and eternal, for they belong to thought. But we must tell our naturalists they cannot play fast and loose with us in this business of atoms. One ingenious scientist[6] has told us, to explain how small they are, that if a drop of water were made as large as the earth, the atoms composing it would be larger than marbles, but not quite as large as cricket-balls ! And these atoms are the ultimate and indivisible. We must really recall our atomistic friends to clear thinking. Just as long as the atom can be conceived at all, whether as " marbles " or "cricket-balls," it must be conceived capable of division into halves, quarters, or any number of fractions. Just as long as the atom is that protean thing, matter, at all, just so long will it play them the tricks of matter.

They must put the atom, as the last result, into the realm of the ideal,—a thing which belongs to the pure intellect ; so only can they be certain of keeping it an atom, in that great day when a drop of water becomes as large as a world !

But why should I dwell upon the uncertainties of material science, when its latest teachers themselves are uncertain whether matter exists at all, when, at all events, even granting its

---

6 Sir William Thompson.

existence, it is out of our power to know any thing about it or even its qualities ; for are we not in a world where we can have only sensations, where all we know are our sensations, and where, at best, we have only a faint sort of right to infer that there may be some thing outside answering to those sensations ?—a "permanent possibility of sensation" at best ? Indeed, in the elaboration of the latest thinking in this direction, the distinguished author[7] seems to be uncertain whether he himself exists, or rather is quite certain he does not. The only thing he is sure of, appears to be, that "the Power behind phenomena is inscrutable."

One therefore may come, I think, without any restraining awe, certainly without any conceited presumption, to ask again of a theory that leads to such uncertain results—whether it is absolutely true, and covers and accounts for all the facts, so that the world just made itself, and keeps on making and unmaking itself, without any maker, and without any reason ? For this, as I said at the beginning is what now claims to be regarded as *science :* that is, that something which is known.

[7] Mr. Herbert Spencer.

It is called evolution in physics, and natural selection, or "survival of the fittest," in
biology.

Now let me say just here that it is folly, and
worse, to speak lightly or disrespectfully of
Mr. Darwin, the keen, careful observer, the
delightful reporter of discoveries, the amiable,
kindly gentleman. That Mr. Spencer, who
is the author of a philosophy which undertakes to explain the universe by evolution,
and who has formulated a series of "laws" by
which the universe makes and unmakes itself,
is the peer of any man living for abstruse
thinking and metaphysic speculation, goes
without saying. How inconclusive I believe
Mr. Darwin's reasoning from his facts, how
wide the gaps he leaves unexplained, how gal-
lantly he imagines where facts fail him, and
how easily he gives up his theory in later editions, or bolsters it with new inventions, do
not, in the slightest, lesson my admiration for
the enthusiastic student of orchids and pigeons,
and the delightful naturalist of the *Beagle*.
That Mr. Spencer reasons most perversely,
as it seems to me; is confused and confusing,
invents a new language, and gives new mean-
ings to old English words; that his conclusions

are irrational and sometimes "unthinkable" (to use a word of his own) ; that he deals freely in "pseud-ideas," and facts which are not facts, does not make him any the less a man of great ability, honest, and honestly working, according to his lights, at explaining, after his fashion, a theory of the universe which he is trying to make coherent, and which will have its day, and pass away among other equally fantastic theories of the universe, which have faded into Prof. Tyndall's "infinite azure of the past."

We have no disrespect for either of these gentlemen when we decline to accept their theories as science, and we beg to say that when their names are mentioned, as they sometimes are, as if that should end all discussion, our awe is not awakened at the sound, nor our opinion of the intellectual capacity of the namers greatly elevated.

The question simply is, Does the theory of evolution account for all the facts ? There is not a man among you, trained to any clear logical thinking, who is not as capable of answering that question as either of these gentlemen. They have no data which you do not possess. The dealing with the data is just

a matter of sound thinking—belongs entirely
to the realm of logic.

But what is the theory? Not merely evolution. In an evolution in nature all students of
nature recognize a familiar fact. Every sprout-
ing seed reveals it. But such evolution is from
the potential to the actual. Every acorn is
an oak in germ. The evolution is by a fixed
law towards a fixed end, according to a fixed
purpose. On definite lines clearly settled by
some intelligence, all things develop or evolve
from the germ. The germ contains the product in potency—contains it perhaps, in fact,
had we eyes to see it.

Under the idea that this is what is meant by
evolution, many Christian men have the notion that they may be evolutionists and Christians also. If God made the world a living
world, a seminarium and seed-bed of things, in
which all things were potentially and to appear
actually in their time, it is about what St. Au-
gustine held, and a goodly catena of the Schol-
astics, including Aquinas. If this were the
reconcilement meant, it might not seem hard
to reconcile science and religion. As the late
Charles Kingsley put it: "We knew of old
that God was so wise that He could make all

things, but behold He is so much wiser than even that, that He can make all things make themselves."

But the doctrine of evolution, as " science " puts it before us, is another thing altogether. According to this, which now calls itself science, and is so understood as an unassailable, determinate conclusion by most ignorant readers, we are required to hold that there is no God to begin with, that there is no Reason and no Will, that no operation in nature has any intelligence or any purpose, that all these makings, and evolutions, so-called, and developments, are merely the surgings and rhythmical heavings of brute matter and brute force, signifying nothing.

The human eye, while being far from perfect, is yet a wonderful and admirable instrument, in comparison with which the most perfect telescope or microscope is a poor clumsy contrivance. But how came the human eye, and for what purpose was it intended? You and I would say, the eye was constructed for the purpose of seeing. That seems to be the only conclusion for sane common-sense, and the healthy action of non-crazy human thinking. But the system which insists upon itself

as " science," which demands that we shall accept more wonders than all the miracles of all
religions, true and false, ancient or modern,
upon the word of one Englishman, tells us
NO! The eye was not made to see by!
There was no purpose of the sort governing
its development! Matter, in an infinite number of trillions of years, by infinite trillions of
happy chances, preserving the beneficial varia-
tions, and letting the unbeneficial die, gradually kept on developing, not knowing what
it wanted, having no sense more than any
lump of mud, until it developed—never meaning to do so—the eye of a philosopher or the
eye of an eagle!

I might be willing to grant Mr. Darwin's
theory as sufficient for the eye of a philosopher, if his theory be philosophy, but I decline
to accept it for the eye of the eagle.[8]

I have not misrepresented nor exaggerated.
The theory of evolution which insists that it is
" science " has to face, among other things, the
question of the eye. It is not by any means
its most puzzling question. But such is the
way it meets it: the eye was not made for

---

[8] See Mr. Darwin's account of the origin of the eye, "Origin of
Species," pp. 222, 226.

the purpose of seeing. That would concede reason, purpose, a brain, and sense in the making of the world, and would annihilate the whole "science," which requires us to believe that in matter alone is the power, potency, and sufficiency of all life and all thought.[9]

I cannot here quote, our time is too short. I just state what is familiar to all readers of what calls itself "science," that the dogma taken for granted, insisted upon as needing no proof, offered for our acceptance as the first step in wisdom, is that there is no meaning, no purpose, no aim, and no end—in short, *no sense* in the universe! The whole system of Mr. Spencer, for instance, formally drawn out and stated, only pretends, in its long-winded Greek compounds, to register what *is.* For myself I do not believe, of course, that it does that, nor anywhere near that. But its foundation principle is that; at its best, that is all it can do. It is precluded from undertaking to tell us the *by whom* and the *why!* undertakes to tell us of the *how* only, and blunders and stutters about that, because it fetters its movement with the two balls and chains of its slavery— there *is* no WHO, and there is no Why!

---

[9] Mr. Darwin, again and again, admits that if any purpose were discoverable—if, for instance, even flowers were *intended* to be beautiful, it would destroy his theory.

Let us clearly understand that before we go one step farther. The thing that calls itself "science," that arrogates that magnificent name in our day, begins with the magisterial assertion that the *how* alone is within our power, and bounds the limit of our thought. How the thing is, it is " scientific " to enquire. Who made it, what is it, and *why* it is what it is, we are told are illegitimate questions. It is a waste of time to ask them. They lead to the inscrutable. That is the only thing certain.

Now with the utmost required and becoming respect for Mr. Spencer, am I to be shut up to the bounds he arbitrarily assigns to human thinking ? The very questions which he puts aside as impossible and senseless—the " from what " and the " why " of things—have been the central questions of thinkers (compared to whom, with all respect to him, he is a babe in arms) since the dawn of recorded thought, and are the central and main questions yet. The *how* is the question of the artist, the arranger, the tabulator, the " scientist " at best ; the " by what " and the " for what " are the questions of the common heart, and the common sense, and the common need, as they are of the deepest philosophy.

But here we touch a very strange fact. The system of evolution, like every other system of philosophy, is an attempt to explain the *rationale* of things. It arises, as all do, from an innate and ever-present demand of the intellect for reasons, for causes, for an order. The principle of causality is imperative in human thinking. There is nothing more so. Consciously or unconsciously it is at work. The boor's mind asserts it, as does the philosopher's. There is no difference, in the *beginning*, between them. The only difference is in the rationality and sense of the conclusions reached. The crudest human thinking turns to the universe about it, and to itself and its life, and demands a whence, a why, and a how. A cause for an effect. The constitution of man is such that he requires a reason for things, and it is to that imperative requirement that he owes all his advancement in knowledge. It is the parent of all his philosophies, sciences, and theologies. The apple falls. But *why* does it fall? Not merely, mark you HOW? for the answer then would simply register a process without satisfactory reason. But *why?* by what cause, and for what purpose?

And here is the great and fatal lack in the

entire system of evolution as a philosophy.[10]
In England alone, possibly, and in shop-keep-
ing England, not the England of Bacon or
Shakespeare, but the England of Cobden and
Bright, could such a system have ventured to
assume the name of philosophy.   True or false,
it is a mere registering of the *how*—the manner of the process.   It scornfully scouts the
idea that we can know the whence or the why,
the cause and the meaning.   There is that sort
of shallow practicality about it which belongs
to buyers and sellers, to the men of cotton-
mills and spinning-jennies, and a farthing better on a bolt of calico and a farthing less on a
cotton bale, to whom no thinking which does not
think out profit is of any use.

And yet, though the master of the system
tells us that there is nothing so certain as that
the *by what* and the *why* are utterly inscrutable, and the pupils tell us that to inquire about
them is a childish waste of time, we are here
met by the curious fact (for human nature is a

---

[10] The evolution philosophy is like the philosophy of the locomotive
which would tabulate the revolution of the wheels, the pressure of
the steam, the consumption of the coal, the number of pieces in the
machinery, while resolutely insisting that the questions " Who made
it?" and " What was it made for ?" are quite impractical—in fact,
"unthinkable."   There is no doubt but a very practical knowledge
—sufficient to run the engine—would be thus acquired.

persistent affair, and cannot be choked by philosophers), that still the old questions *are* put ; that even they themselves, whether or no, must put them ; and that their entire philosophies are attempts to make the universe an ordered kosmos, to make it respectably sensible and rational to human thought.

And first of all, if the philosophy be true ; if, by the blind working of blind force, man and man's brain and man's sense and reason come out of slime without any purpose ; if in all the infinite ages past there was no sense and no aim, but only an infinite set of chances ; how comes it that this senseless and purposeless power evolves a being who turns round and demands of it *how* it came to do this, and by what power and for what end ?   How came a senseless force to evolve a sensible man ?   An irrational brute movement to create a reason ?   A thing that cannot put two and two together to evolve a creature who turns round on this thing, criticises its action, blames its processes, demands to know its meaning, writes "First Principles" and other philosophic books about it, drags it bound to his bar of judgment, and when its workings do not suit him, checks or upsets those workings at his will ?

For you understand, of course, that by this philosophy there is but one force in heaven above or earth beneath ; that it is the same force driving on to mad ruin in the cyclone of the western prairie, and in the mother's voice singing her babe to sleep in the cottage in its path ; that in the rotting swamp that breeds the pestilence, where foul things twist and crawl, and the heavy air bears poisonous death, the force is just the same as that which weaves the lofty measures of " The Idyls of the King," or writes Mr. Herbert Spencer's " First Principles,"—as much sense and purpose in it at one time as another.

I fail to see how the rational can come out of the irrational. To me the conception is " unthinkable "—an utterly " pseud-idea," to use pet phrases. I simply cannot commit the intellectual suicide which requires me to believe that a thing like the eye of an eagle was not made, but produced through trillions of years by millions of happy chances, which chanced to survive, and that it was not intended in any of those millions of years as a thing to see by. I must decline to be scolded out of my common-sense in the name of " science."

If I find a piece of chipped flint, a poor, clumsy little bit of stone hacked into a rude triangular form, there is not a living scientist that will not tell me "that was made by a man, a rational man, and it had a final end; it was meant for shooting with." Yet I find so marvellous a structure as the human eye, and a great scientist has a great intellect so twisted by the worship of his "idols of the cave," that he tells me it was never made, and it certainly *was not* evolved for the purpose of seeing!

I think no reflecting man can fail to be struck with the position man occupies upon the earth in regard to this matter. He demands that the world shall give an account of itself—shall be a *sane* world. By his mental constitution he is compelled to believe there is a cause for what he sees and a purpose in things. The world is not a mad-house. Things go by rule. And on that conviction man masters the world. For, when he finds things unreasonable, he sets to work rationalizing them. He dikes in the river; he drains the marsh; he fells the forest; he walls out the sea. He blasts the hills open and bursts his way into the mine. He removes mountains, as was promised, by faith—faith in his own sense, and in the world's sense also. He has modified the face of the earth in the historic period—that is, in the time in which we know any thing about him, or the world either —more than all blind forces, tides, winds, earthquakes, together."

Every step he takes is based upon the conviction that there is *sense* in things which will answer to his sense, that the world made by a Logos will respond to the dealings of a Logos, that brains somehow fit in with the management of the world, and that its force, in any shape, can be understood by brains, managed and even mastered by brains.

The poets, who express the inmost heart and root of things, by that insight which makes them seers, and with the central truth which makes them teachers and sages, have never doubted about a world with sense, a world made for something, good for something.

In every drama of Shakespeare the scene is in a world where the laws are laws with a meaning and laws with an end. From Sophocles and Euripides to Alfred Tennyson, the

---

" See " The Earth as Modified by Human Action," by George P. Marsh.

poets, like the real philosophers, do not fear to tell us of a world that has a meaning.

That " one increasing purpose runs
Through all the circles of the suns,"

has been the faith of all the intellectual guides of men. The mind rejects the teachers of blindness, senselessness, and chaos coming again.

I stand in amazement, at times, before the attitude of these men, who demand of me intellectual suicide in this matter of final causes. Such a man as Sir Henry Thompson, for instance, is so paralyzed by the temporary scientific fashion, so stands in awe of a form of words, that he feels compelled to apologize, because, in a late article, he ventures to suggest that the decay of the teeth in old age might signify that the old man need not eat so much beef and mutton as formerly !

Here, in an institution of liberal learning, I may surely plead for intellectual liberty, against the fetters of a system which would impose itself under the name of science without scientific proof.

Mr. Darwin finds that under domestication and the care of men, plants and animals, pi-

geons especially, will take on peculiar forms.
At the same time the pigeons are always
pigeons, never become eagles, nor even geese.
Also, as soon as this intelligent oversight is
removed, the evidence is, that, left to his own
devices, all the peculiarities will disappear, and
tumbler and fantail and pouter will become
rock pigeons like their grandmothers.  So far
*science*.  That much we *know*.

But from this, to assume that, without intelligent control, by happy-go-lucky chance,
which happened to fit, and happened to stay,
not the varieties of species, but the infinite
varieties of all known things, animal and vege-
table, the toad-stool and the toad, the sage-
bush and the sage, the blind-worm and William
Shakespeare, all came from the same grandfather, and evolved themselves somehow—
nobody knows how, in some place—nobody
knows where, in some time—nobody knows
when, and by the power of a formula, namely,
"survival of the fittest," from the same original mud-bath, I humbly beg to believe is not
science, and scarce a rational guess, to the
thought of men whose brains are yet normal.

For there is not in all the historic period, in
all the records of all the past wherein men

lived, nor in any bones dug up in any place, a single case in evidence where a cat became a dog, an oyster ever became a clam, or an oak tree became a chestnut tree. So far are we from evidence that a sponge was the kosmic grandfather of Plato.

I am not concerned to dwell here upon the enormous difficulties, the unbridged gaps, the wild guesses, and bald assumptions with which the amiable naturalist weaves his romance, nor even to call attention to the fact that in his last editions he has practically given up the position of the first. These things are all treated of abundantly by scientific men, and will be hereafter.

I am dealing here with the central idea of Mr. Darwin, organized into his philosophy by Mr. Spencer, that in all these changes there is *no sense.* The logical lapse is enormous. The only changes, marked and striking (but within the bounds of species), are of animals and plants in *domestication*, under control of reason and will, modifying and even opposing nature ; and Mr. Darwin's logical conclusion is, that when he finds changes, not under domestication, he is to assume there is no reason and no will in the case !

The pouter pigeon, in so far as he differs
from the other pigeons, does so because a
rational will and purpose controls him and
keeps him a pouter, indeed made him a
pouter in the first place for reasons of its own.
Mr. Darwin hence concludes that the pigeon
himself was made without any rational will or
intention, and stays a pigeon for no reason or
end whatever.  You may call this " science,"
for people talk very loosely nowadays ; but,
gentlemen, you have studied logic—is it
logic ?

Years and generations of careful training
with a specific purpose, by a rational will, has
succeeded in making a setter dog.  It has not
made a horse of him, and the idea that it
could, even if carried to the end of time, would
be considered a very " pseud-idea " indeed.
The dog has not shown the slightest tendency
even to become a fox or a wolf.  He is still a
dog.  But he is a particular type of dog, with
particular tendencies and capacities, which are
kept cultivated and intended for a specific
purpose.  Let him go his own way, and, in a
few generations, left to nature, your highbred
setter is a mongrel cur, making night hideous
with the dogs of Constantinople.

Now shall I be told that while it requires reason, fixed purpose, and the sensible management of a controlling will, to keep and preserve the small variation which makes the setter, since it will disappear if the setter is turned loose to nature's care, yet the enormous variation, which differentiates the entire dog from a dogwood blossom, was brought about without any reason, or any sense, or any will, and for no purpose?

Mind, this is not even questioning that the dog may be the product of Bathybius. It is only asking, if it takes some sense, will, and purpose to make a setter out of a cur, and keep him setter, whether it is rational, logical, and highly scientific to conclude that it took no will, no purpose, no rational sense to make a dog out of Bathybius, and keep him a dog?

The scientific people have their own work in this business, and some of them are attending to it as they ought to do. They are showing the facts distorted, the theories assumed as facts, the staring facts put aside, the evidence built on guesses and *a priori* assumptions which have no place in natural science, and which every man has the inherent right to make for himself, and every other man has the inherent right to deny!

But here we have only time to point to the perversions of logic, which are perhaps not to be wondered at in a system which begins by denying any logic in the universe.

Take the very definition of evolution as applied to biology : natural selection—survival of the fittest. Selection of what ? Survival of what?

Mr. Darwin holds that man's immediate ancestor was a monkey, arboreal in his habits (lived in trees, that is), was covered with hair, and had a tail. Now, some monkey of this breed took a step some time toward becoming a man. What was it ? He must have come down out of the trees ! He must have determined to stop being monkey to the degree of walking on his hind legs ! He must have taken some method to gradually get rid of his tail !

Now, notice, the long forearms, the claws, the prehensile tail, had been, by Mr. Darwin's theory, developed to enable the creature to live in trees. He and his survived, according to Mr. Spencer, because, having such tails, claws, four feet, which were not hands and not feet either, thick skulls, little brain, and consequently light heads, and hairy bodies, they were best fitted to live in trees.

And now the first adventurous monkey who has the ambition to become a man, foregoes all these advantages, insists on tottering on his hinder legs and disusing his tail ; insists on coming down out of the trees where he could gather nuts, escape stronger animals, swing by his tail, and curl up warm in his fur ; insists on throwing away his advantages as a quite admirable monkey, and becoming a very imbecile, idiotic, and helpless man. Why, such a monkey would have been torn limb from limb the first day by some wildcat. He would have starved to death because he would not climb for nuts. He would have been pelted to death in derision of his folly by his own companions. In some one of a hundred wretched ways our supposed ambitious ancestor would have perished—when he had given up all his advantages as a monkey, and had not acquired a single advantage as a man !

Seriously, I mean, that just here is a logical gulf which is impassable. What the developing monkey gained, to enable him to survive as the fittest, must have been in the direction of making him a complete monkey—never in the direction of making him like a fish or like a man.

What enables the dog to survive on the principle, if it be a principle, of survival of the fittest, must be that he becomes in some direction more of a dog. No possible development of a trout, in the direction of survival of the fittest, would ever make the trout successful on dry land. If the theory of some modern biologists, that birds are the descendants of snakes, were true (which I do not, of course, believe), it surely must find it hard to place itself under the laws of development. The snake, whose prey is to be seized by gliding noiselessly upon it, without disturbance of leaf or branch or dry twig (if he be a tree-climbing snake), must have strangely embarrassed his proceedings by fluttering and plunging about with his useless embryo wings, to the alarm of the whole forest—wings he could not fly with yet, and which spoiled his shape for creeping. He lost his advantage of fitness as a snake, and had acquired no advantage yet as a bird !

And that is the difficulty in the combination of these two theories, which are strangely confounded, while they are totally separate and even mutually destructive.

" Survival of the fittest " has nothing to do

with creation of species. Indeed, its operation, if one examine, would be to render mutation of species impossible. Each soldier in the struggle for existence handles his own weapon best. The eagle survives as the fittest eagle. No fitness as an eagle makes him likely to survive as a swan. That which makes the horse survive is the excellence of the qualities which make him a horse—a lion's claws, an eagle's wings, a whale's fins, would not help him. And that which makes the monkey survive, is that he is a capable, shrewd, cunning, flexible-handed, and flexible-spined monkey. He survives because his development is on the line of monkey-development, and he is the fittest monkey to exist. Any attempt to imitate a man, to put clothes upon himself, to walk on two hands, to stand erect, to do without those big jaws which crack the nuts, or to get a bigger brain which would make him giddy,—all this would not help him to be a man, and would be his utter ruin as a monkey.

So enormous is the gap to be bridged that Mr. Wallace (who wrought out the theory of natural selection about the same time as Mr. Darwin, and quite independently) cannot bring himself to include man in its working. Mr. Darwin, however, more logically, includes him,—and, indeed, if the blind chances of matter vibrating from homogeneous to heterogeneous is able to account for all the rest of the universe, one need not stop at man !

Yet man is the completion—the crown of all the selection, and all the survival, according to the theory.   And there is this curious consequence.   Not only his existence, but his life, his words, his works, his thoughts, his affections, must all be accounted for by the action of force.   You must look to weigh his love and hate by foot-pounds, as you weigh any other manifestation of force.   His patriotism, his sense of justice, his benevolence, must be expressible in the units of the metric system. His most elevated religious feeling, his tenderest human sentiment, must be expressible in measures of force.   You must be prepared to accept the thought of a Shakespeare or a Bacon, as the equivalent of the force, that fats a swine or makes a dunghill rot !

It is necessary at times to take matters out of the veil of learned phrases in which they are concealed, and put them in simple English, that we may understand.   The result I

have mentioned is accepted by the philosophy
of evolution, on its so-called law of the
correlation and conservation of force : a
Principia manifests the same force which fats
a bullock ; and a Hamlet, the force that rots
him by the roadside should you leave him
there. All is from molecular motion, and
there is as much sense in one set of vibrations
as in another ! But here again comes in the
*I* of man,—the will, the personality, the
self-assertion. Define him as you will, and
theorize about his coming as you will, here
man is, with a reason, and he demands that
nature must be rational. He declines to sub-
mit to any thing he judges irrational. If
matter has developed him by any rule of
thumb, like survival of the fittest, he acts
very strangely toward his Creator.

He turns right about on nature, and says, I,
and not you, shall decide what and who is
fittest. You say weeds, I say corn. You say
cockle, I say wheat. You say wolves, I say
sheep. You say hawks, I say doves. What I
consider fittest, shall survive in spite of you ;
and your fittest, which you are trying with all
your powers to preserve, shall perish at my
word. You have used your utmost to make

the swamp survive.    Lo, I say it shall perish !
To make the tangled forest survive, and, lo I
destroy it, and the fair geen meadow survives
it its stead.

Has survival of the fittest developed then its
own master ?   It would seem so.   There is no
way to explain these things away and leave
the universal common-sense of men existing.

Mr. Huxley is compelled to admit that our
" will counts for something in the course of
events."   If it counts for any thing, it traverses
fatally the philosophy of development.   But
men's common sense, and common eyesight,
and common consciousness, tell them it counts
for more on the face of this world than all
other forces whatever.   It dares to dash itself
right up against the bucklers of blind force,
and demand a reason.   It compels an explanation, and asserts the mastery of the will and the
Logos, the Light and the Life, by breaking
the blind forces into harness, and driving them
by that will.

All other creatures seem parts of nature,
live dumbly in accord with its dumb forces,
question nothing either in life or in death.
This last strange creature, in passionate protest
against mere force, against disorder, confusion,

and unreason, stands defying the universe, and insisting that if it be not rational, he is bound to make it rational, and will make it so, or die protesting and armed upon the field.

"Survival of the fittest," is it? Who *are* fittest? What does nature know about it; or "natural selection," when it comes to man? He shall decide, I say. His hunch-back child shall survive as Alexander Pope, and write Dunciads and Essays on Man. His poor puny offspring shall survive as Isaac Newton, to tell the world how its Maker hangs the stars in order, and rolls the systems in harmony. His purblind scrufulous son shall be Dr. Samuel Johnson. His blind men shall see Iliads and Odyssies arise from the many-sounding sea, or their sightless eyes shall pierce the heavens with Milton, and scan the secrets of the abyss. His weakling, doomed to perish by your blind law of survival, shall stand upon the quarter-deck of the *Victory* and guide the thunders of Trafalgar. Man shall measure, by his own judgment of fitness, his own children; and the weakest of them, physically, shall be his heroes and his leaders, his lords of men and shakers of the world.

For here when we have scanned the field,

we are brought back to the old proclamation
of reason : " In the beginning was the Logos,
all things were made by Him, and without Him
was not any thing made that was made."

And man, the image of the Logos, finite,
shadow of the Eternal and Infinite Reason,
stands facing nature on his royal right to question, to order, to modify, to control ; stands
to vindicate, by his position of reason, the
universe as no Devil's phantasmagoria, no
beastly lair of Setebos and Caliban, but a
world of order and of law, where all is reasonable as far as we have yet seen, and in which
our human instinct keeps time and touch so
true to the Nature of Things, that we stride
forward as if under an overpowering com-
mand, to demand that it shall be rational, and
that we must make it rational whereinsoever
it fails.

I hold that the attitude of humanity, in this
respect, upon the earth has no logical basis, and
no sufficient scientific basis, save that, being a
world of reason, will, and purpose, this creature
of reason, will, and purpose feels it is his own,
that it fits him and answers to him, and that
every step in the process of making it a human
world, is another step in the making it divine.

# LECTURE SECOND.

" They fought from Heaven.
The stars in their courses fought against Sisera."
—JUDGES, v., 20.

A CRY from a woman's lips—a triumphant cry for a great national deliverance. The right cause and the wrong had met, as they have met so often on the world's battle-fields, and, on this field at least, the wrong went down, while, to outward seeming, the right was feeble and the wrong was strong.

Cruelty, oppression, brute power, with its chariots of iron and its serried ranks of spears, met a hastily gathered band who fought for home and freedom and order and right, and as at Platea and Marathon, and on many a smitten field beside, the right was victor, to the lasting joy of men.

And this strange woman, prophetess and poet, judge and leader, who had summoned the army of the defenders, sang to the listening sky her song of triumph for her people.

43

The victory was so complete, the defeat was so overwhelming, that, praise as she might, as they well deserved, Barak ben Abinoam and his ten thousand, the event was not thus explainable.

Merely human forces were not sufficient. The victory came from the unseen powers. The eternal righteousness that stands behind the shadow of every temporal wrong had taken the cause into his own hands. "They fought from heaven. The stars in their courses fought against Sisera." The awful powers of nature were against this evil man and the brutally selfish kingdom he defended. "The nature of things" showed itself on the side of righteousness.

Is this the rhapsody of an excited poetical imagination only? Consider that the poet's truth is always the highest human truth. For he sees the heart of things, the unchanging reality under the ever-changing show. The truest human book in the English tongue is that which contains the poems of Shakespeare. Newton's Principia is not truer than Macbeth.

But this woman was seer and poet in one. She had not only sight, but insight. She sang that the stars might hear. She sang for all the ages. And because her utterance was true forever, the utterance in Hebrew speech of an everlasting law, her song could not die as a song of mere patriotic rejoicing ; but echoes under all the skies and surges up to all the stars, a world's proclamation : "The stars in their courses fought against Sisera."

One cannot help remembering the lonely soul, gnawing his heart in pain, grimly wrestling with sickness of body and that *sæva indignatio* that tortured the soul of Swift—the scorn and hatred against a mean, cowardly, and stupid world,—who has just passed from among us, and how passionately he clung to this, when there was nothing else to cling to ; how he made himself its prophet, and proclaimed it fiercely sometimes, sometimes pathetically and mournfully, that the "eternal veracities," at least, were always on the side of right and armed against wrong ;—Thomas Carlyle from Scottish hill-side or crowded London street proclaiming, as best he might, the law that burned upon the lips of Deborah four thousand years ago !

I asked in my first lecture, Is the world a rational world ? I ask now, Is it moral ? First, Is there any *sense* in the nature of things, any

intelligence, any purpose or meaning ? And
now I ask, Is there any *right* in the nature of
things or any wrong ?

Deborah's cry is the answer of the Old Testament. It is no discord there. The universal
utterance of seer and prophet, psalmist and his-
torian, is in accord with the voice of her "who
dwelt beneath the palm-tree." "The nature
of things," the awful powers seen and unseen,
are against wrong. The blood of a murdered
brother cries from the ground. The earth will
not hide the murder. The heavens will become
brass and the earth iron when men turn to
evil. The burden of the ancient book from
first to last is a proclamation that the forces of
nature avenge the poor and the unjustly
oppressed, and are armed against the tyrant
and the evil-doer, and the end is certain in due
time. These Hebrew words of threatened
vengeance against lies, hypocrisy, cowardice,
selfishness, and wrong, are, when you examine
them, in their most terrific denunciations, but
the proclamation that the world is moral, the
kosmos is on the side of righteousness, the
stars and spaces and abysses above, below, are
against the evil, are forever rolling the right
into light and victory.

The view of material nature in the New Testament is, as we might expect, an illumination and revelation of the Old.

In our Lord's parables nature puts on a diviner dress. I wonder shall we ever dare in our theologies to think of nature as our Lord saw her? With Him the world is spiritual. Matter is translucent with the light divine. The grass at His feet grows in its way, as the archangels grow in theirs. The sparrow's law is a concentric circle with the laws that bind Orion and the Pleiads. The country laborer scattering seed in the furrow, the philosopher that sows thought, the preacher that scatters principles among men,—even the eternal Logos and Son of Man Himself who drops living words into the seed-bed of men's souls, work on a continuous line, under one law, whose circuit sweeps the infinite.

Facing this doctrine of Revelation stands the doctrine of what is called "Science." Here again there is absolutely no reconciliation. Evolution, as a system of ethics, declares the universe not *im*moral indeed, for that would be to give it some spiritual value, but absolutely *un*moral. The moral qualities of men, like the intellect of men, are the result of

molecular vibrations. By a law of fatal necessity, the same force that acts in the brain and
arm of the murderer, acts also in the brain and
heart of the tenderest mother that watches
over her baby's cradle. The action in each
case is, in the last analysis, absolutely indifferent, even absolutely the same.

What we call morality is only the result of
inherited molecular movement in the brain.
There is no absolute right or wrong in the
case, none in the world, no ultimate " I ought,"
anywhere, and the whole kosmos which has
been evolved by the rhythmic vibrations of the
atoms is absolutely indifferent to rights and
wrongs.

You will observe that the system does not
deny that there are such words as right and
wrong, and that they represent *something*.
But what they represent is purely conventional
—the notions that have been formed by hered-
ity, by the law of the survival of the fittest, in
men trying to live together in a social order.

They have no value, I mean, outside of the
environment. They are not of the essence or
necessity of things—these ideas of right and
wrong. There is nothing answering to them
in the universe. They have been evolved out

of matter and will fall back like every thing else into the homogeneity of the world-mist again, the weltering chaos of gases, which is the same stuff out of which are made all virtues and all goodnesses, all lovelinesses and tendernesses, as well as all lusts and all beastlinesses, all swine and all sties for swine.

I desire to put the conclusion which is accepted, and even gloried in, by the masters in this school, into the plainest English, that we see it for what it is—something that is apt to escape us when left in the large and learnedly sounding syllables of "science!"

Now let us observe here that no matter what may be the explanation of, the origin of, the ideas of right and wrong, the fact of their existence in man is admitted of necessity. The doctrine of evolution requires that they shall have been evolved from the original cell like all else, and were latent and potential in the hypothetical fire-mist of the nebular theory. But the theorist is bound to admit their present existence as much as you or I. He is of course also bound to show how they gradually grew to be what they are in a Christian man, in the saintliest soul that ever blessed the world, in our Lord Himself (let us state the conclusion without a word of the horror it inspires), through crawling worm, lemur, and ape and brutal savage—the same in all, and in their activity in all just the same —the blind quiverings, the attractions and repulsions of matter!

But the fact is that here is a being who has a conscience, as we call it, as well as a consciousness. Barbarous or civilized, in the Feejee Islands or in London, it is all the same : this unique being has the sense of right and wrong, goodness and badness, differ as he may about his classification of those qualities.

It is the power to make a moral judgment I am speaking of, not at all the manner in which such judgment acts. The lameness of the explanation of evolution is that it misses the real point here, or ignores. From animal instincts and from hereditary influences after the beast developed into a man, from the blind gropings of a creature trying to survive in his environment, it might be not a vagary of the scientific imagination to hold that a notion of certain things as bad and certain things as good might arise. As one of our wisest has said : " The ox, if he could think, would call the grazier a good man because he feeds oxen, and the butcher a bad man because he slaughters them."

Therefore it is that evolution must deny any absolute morality at all. Moral notions are the growth of the struggle for existence, like all else. In themselves they have no moral value. If we attribute such value, it is a delusion which also comes from pure selfishness on our part, because the good man's acts are profitable to us. Altruism, which is the highest test of evolutionary morality, is only good because civilized man cannot survive in the struggle for existence unless he gives others a chance. Pleasure, therefore, is, after all, the necessary root of all morality. Pleasure is the only absolutely good thing, and pain the only absolutely evil. It is of course impossible to found absolute morality on a sensation. But, indeed, I need scarcely dwell so long on this, since the theory denies that there is any thing absolute except matter and force—if indeed they be two and not one—and both are alike unknowable.[1]

---

[1] I have avoided speaking of the very ugly practical consequences which grow out of the doctrine of evolution, when it is applied to ethics. I may quote a Scotchman and a German to show the fruitfulness of the doctrine and the nature of the fruit.

The Scotch professor, Alexander Bain, in a lecture on the

But we have to face a fact which I hesitate
not to say is universal in man, and which makes
him unique among living beings on the earth,
—the fact, namely, that he has the power of
exercising moral judgments, and that he
habitually exercises them ; that this power is
just as plainly his as the power of sight or the
power of reflection ; that its habitual exercise is
one of his most ordinary activities ; that he is a

"Correlation of Nervous and Mental Forces," reprinted in a volume
of Appleton's "Scientific Series," remarks of excitement : "It is not
*a final* end of our being, as pleasure is." The equivalent of this
is repeated more than once. Prof. Bain does not seem to be aware
that there is any doubt that pain is the sole evil and pleasure the
sole good.

But the most curious result of his medley of matter and mind
occurs in this sentence. He is speaking of the consumption of
Force in "moral acquisitions" :

"The carefully poised estimate of good and evil for self, the ever-
present sense of the interests of others, and the ready obedience to
all the special ordinances that make up the morality of the time,
however truly expressed in terms of high and abstract spiritu-
ality, have their counterpart in the physical organism. They have
used up a large and definite amount of nutriment, and had they been
*less developed* there would have been *a gain* of power to some other
department, mental or physical."

That is, the man without a conscience has an advantage mentally
or physically ! He is much more likely to "succeed" ! And
benevolence, conscientiousness, piety uses up a "definite amount of
nutriment (measurable in foot-pounds) which might have gone to
making a fortune or winning a prize-fight.

When "moral philosophy" lands us here, the end of that species of
it is not far off.

Prof. Ed. V. Hartmann in his "Philosophy of the Unknown" has

moral being as plainly as he is a seeing or reflecting being.

The question is not how came he to have
such and such moral opinions—they may be
right or wrong,—but how came he to have
moral insight at all? Whence, in a blind
world of mere atomic quiverings, came a being who, apart from all questions of force and
all questions of pleasure, in addition to all other

---

a more cynical frankness than his Scotch brother of the same school.
He says : " It is important to make beast life better known to youth
as being the truest source of pure nature, wherein they may learn to
understand *their true being* in its simplest form, and, in it, *rest and
refresh themselves*, after the artificiality and deformity of our social
condition."

Again : " Let us only think how agreeably an *ox* or a *hog* lives,
almost as if he had learned to do so from Aristotle !"

And why not ? As long as he has enough to eat, and a good place
to wallow, he is " in harmony with his own environment "—Mr.
Spencer's idea of a perfect condition,—and is seeking faithfully what
Mr. Bain teaches is the true end, not only of the hog's existence, but
of the existence of the hog's Darwinian cousins, for whom Mr. B.
lectures,—pleasure ! Queer doctrine in the Scotland of John Knox !

To clear the atmosphere after this, let us have a blast of fresh air
from the heather. Let " true Thomas," the one Scottish writing-
man of our time, say *his* say :

" Has the word ' Duty ' no meaning ? Is what we call Duty no
Divine messenger and guide, but a false earthly phantasm made up
of desire and fear ? Is the heroic inspiration we name Virtue, but
some passion, some bubble of the blood, bubbling in the direction
others *profit* by ? [altruism of Mr. Spencer]. I know not, only this
I know : If what thou namest Happiness be our true aim, then are
we all astray. Behold thou art fatherless, outcast, and the universe
is—*the Devil's*."

decisions, has that in him which decides a thing
to be right or wrong ?

There is here a question to which I may say
in all calmness no proximately adequate answer
has been attempted by our science. I say this
in the face of Mr. Spencer's "Psychology,"
Mr. Darwin's "Descent of Man," and Prof.
Bain on "The Emotions and the Will."

For the idea of the right and the idea of the
useful are fundamentally distinct. Indeed,
the moral judgment requires for its highest
commendation of an action that it should *not*
be useful nor pleasurable, nor in any way of
benefit to the doer. Mr. Darwin teaches that
the moral sense comes from the development
of such instincts as are possessed by brutes—
by natural selection. The entire school of
sensationalists tell us that right and wrong are
only, in last analysis, pleasure and pain, advantages and disadvantages.

Yet Mr. John Stuart Mill does not hesitate
to write : "If I am informed that the world is
ruled by a Being whose attributes are infinite,
but what they are we cannot learn, nor what
the principles of his government, except that
the highest human morality which we are
capable of conceiving does not sanction them,

convince me of it, and I will bear my fate as I may. But when I am told I must believe this, and at the same time call this being by the names which express and affirm the highest human morality, I say, in plain terms, that I will not. Whatever power such a being may have over me, there is one thing which he shall not do, he shall not compel me to worship him. I will call no being good who is not what I mean when I apply that epithet to my fellow-creatures, and if such a being can sentence me to hell, to hell I will go."

The sentiment of the believer in absolute right and wrong could not be more strongly or better expressed. It is not a question of profit, or pleasure, or advantage. The human soul stands upon its moral dignity and declares that no power shall make it surrender itself to be the slave of the evil, and no inducement make it lie to its own nature and call that evil good.

Mr. Mill bears witness to the rooted intuition which no false theories can destroy out of humanity. He bears witness as well to the identity and permanence of that intuition as a part of human nature, when he, the Englishman, repeats in English what was a Roman

utterance centuries ago : " Victrix causa placuit
diis sed victa Catoni." Nay, no sophistries, no
theorizing, no juggle of long words, and no
explaining away will rid us of this persistent
fact, that among men in all lands and times
there has been this gift of moral judgment,
this prompt readiness to make it about one's
self and others, this conviction that, when
made, men would understand it, and if true
would accept it, and that such judgment has
appealed to an absolute morality which stands
apart from pleasure or pain, from profit or
loss. "*Fiat justitia ruat cœlum*," is a maxim
that the moral sense accepts universally, and
the loftiest and grandest right act is the act
out of which only sorrow, pain, and loss must
come to the doer.

Here again man turns to nature and asserts
his sovereignty. Produced from matter and
force like the beast or the grass-blade, according to the evolution hypothesis, he turns on
the power that produced him and demands its
meaning, orders it to the bar of his causality
and asks it for an account of itself. But, also,
he summons it before the court of his conscience and demands to know whether it is
moral or immoral, whether its working is right

or wrong, whether it can answer for itself not
only to a being who asks : " Have you any
sense ?" but to a being who asks also : " Have
you any righteousness ?"

Testifying to the permanence and imma-
nence of this moral conviction of an absolute
righteousness in the face of his own poor theories, behold Mr. Mill again arraigning all
nature, without a thought that on his principles he is merely nature's product, like his
own cabbages, and, as judge, condemning her.
That arraignment and that judgment, in his
" Posthumous Essays," stands a memorable
triumph of the existence and persistence of
fact over the finest-spun theories, and an example of the kingly position the human soul
instinctively takes in facing all powers outside
itself in this realm the Father gave his children.

" The order of nature, so far as it is un-
modified by man, is such as no being, whose
attributes are justice and benevolence, would
have made with the intention that his rational
creatures should follow it as an example."

" The ways of nature are to be conquered,
not obeyed. Her powers are often toward
man in the position of enemies."

" If the artificial is not better than the natural, to what end all the arts of life ?   To dig, to plough, to build, to wear clothes, are direct infringements of the injunction to follow nature.   All praise of civilization, or art, or contrivance, is so much dispraise of nature."

And this, a direct blow and a staggering, delivered with another purpose, to be sure, straight in the face of the physical fatalism of Mr. Darwin and Mr. Spencer : " If action could at all be justified, it would only be in direct obedience to instincts, since these might be accounted part of the spontaneous order of nature, but to do any thing with forethought and purpose would be a violation of that perfect order."

I may quote just here Mr. Spencer's rejoicing over the utter absence of moral freedom, and his acceptance of that moral condition which Mr. Mill recoils from in horror.

" I will only further say that freedom of the will, did it exist, would be at variance with the beneficent necessity displayed in the evolution of the correspondence between the organism and the environment. * * * Were the inner relations partly determined by some other agency, the harmony at any moment existing would be disturbed, and the advance to a higher harmony impeded. There would be a retardation of that grand progress which is bearing humanity onward to a higher intelligence and a nobler character."

One moment only upon this to plumb the ethical philosophy of evolution. If there were free will, free moral choice, so that the man tempted to murder had his "inner relations partly determined by some other agency" (conscience, for instance, instilled moral principles, or any other check), which would "disturb the harmony" of the environment (place, time, secret opportunity) which leads him to murder, "there would be a retardation of the grand progress which is bearing humanity onward," etc !

I have not quoted this to show the immorality of the ethical philosophy which the evolution hypothesis necessarily evolves, and the complete blindness of a virtuous man to the consequences of his own theories and the meaning of his own words, for certainly Mr. Spencer has not the remotest idea that his philosophy is immoral, and has expressed his surprise that it should so appear to any. I have quoted to show, as in the case of Mr. Mill, that men

never hesitate to make moral decisions, although their theories require them to deny the
existence of any absolute morality, and even
the existence of any moral distinctions.

Mr. Spencer does not hesitate to call things
" beneficent," to speak of them as " grand " and
" high " and " noble," as if these qualities had
real existence, and as if man had the unques-
tionable power to decide in what they existed,
could recognize and define them by some standard universally acknowledged by human judgment.    To him the order of nature is grand,
noble, and beneficent.    To Mr. Mill it is cruel,
inhuman, and to be opposed by men.    Each
cites the order of nature to the bar of his conscience as he does to the bar of his intellect, and
decides upon its morals as upon its rationality.

Now evidently the standard of the morality
must be like the standard of rationality, outside
nature which is tried and outside the judges
who try it.    It must be an independent and
absolute standard in the minds of both, otherwise there could be no certainty that the ethical judgment or its grounds, or even the words
which express it, would be understood by their
readers.    Each is confident of an ethical judgment in himself, and recognizes, by making it,
its existence in all other men.

But he not only does this, but holds this ethical judgment in humanity to be so sovereign and royal that it is capable of deciding, and by right does try and decide, the moral character of the universe, and its order, and, by consequence, the moral character of its maker— whether you call him the Father Almighty, or " the Power behind phenomena ! "

And these writers are only doing what all writers have been doing, since there were writers at all ; indeed, what all men have been doing since we know they have been doing any thing.

Take out of the world's literatures all that relates to moral questions, and the shelves of our libraries would be bare indeed. I do not mean the books which formally deal with ethics merely. I mean that books like life are saturated with the ethical principle. All great writers are necessarily ethical writers. The moral question, the persistent " I ought," is as prominent in Shakespeare and Dante as if they were formal moralists.

It cannot be otherwise. Nothing is so pressing upon men as the question of what " ought to be," ought to be done, ought to be said, and ought to be the result of the doing and saying. The poets are full of it, the novelists are full

of it, as well as the codes and the religions.
Forever in all his relations the question of the
duty, the thing *due*, the thing he ought, the
thing he *owes* in such and such circumstances,
is a living and pressing question among men.
One of the vastest sides of his intellectual activity, of his organized intellectual occupation,
in government, legislation, courts, codes,
judges, sheriffs, jails, and gibbets, has been,
and is, engaged upon the question of "the
ought." And whatever the theoretical moral
philosopher may elaborate or teach, there is no
doubt in the literatures of man, no doubt in
the moral judging activities of men, no doubt
in the practical decisions of men about their
own acts or the acts of others, that there is an
independent morality beyond them, a law outside themselves, which takes no account of
profit, of survival, or non-survival, which is
self-contained, autocratic, final ; which, when
you get its utterance, gives a decision from
which, by men or gods, there is no appeal,
for *duty* is "stern daughter of the voice of
God." [2]

---

[2] So essentially living, human, overgrowing, is the ethical question,
that the natural philosopher, as we see, becomes a moralist. A
mechanical student discusses the question of duty, a merely physical
science unconsciously passes over into moral science ; and Dr.

Conscience may mistake the utterance, as the bodily ear may mistake a word. But there *is* an eternal " I ought," and man recognizes its existence instinctively, and confesses that it binds supremely, come what may.

Thus appealing to testimony there is no innate conviction so universally confessed by all tongues, pens, and processes of life as that right and wrong are eternal, and that man owes himself to the right.

The grandeur and the nobleness of human character stand, by universal consent, on this loyalty. The iron crown of duty is the imperial crown of human nature. The highest character is that so faithful to the " ought " that all one has, all one is, estate, honors, peace, comfort, name, fame, life itself, shall be surrendered rather than the right be shamed. " Integrity " we call this loyalty to righteousness, and testify, by the word, that it is the wholeness and completeness of human nature. In our ideal of true manhood we demand it : that all shall perish, rather than that right and

---

Huxley in his lecture on " The Physical Basis of Life," while sneering at all the metaphysical and ethical philosophies, as well as at all religions, as vain and useless, proceeds to lay down an ethical science himself, and tell mankind what they " ought " to do, and what " is their plain duty," with all the authority of a Scribe or Pharisee.

truth shall fail.   In slavery, in bonds, in the
dungeon, in disease and rags, in writhing tor-
ture, no man is ruined, no man is shamed or
lost, who stands to the thing that is just and
right.   He keeps his "integrity," his wholeness of manhood, his worth and virtue as a
man, while loyal to righteousness.

The two wonders that filled the soul of
Kant, "the starry heavens above and the
moral law within," were each to him real
alike.   I must accept the universal conviction
that they are alike real to all thinking men—
and almost alike independent of one's self—in
the thinking.

Now this moral law within, this moral judgment and ethical faculty in man, call it what
one may, has never been satisfactorily traced
to any physical origin, notwithstanding the
strange attempts so to trace it.   It remains
a strange portent on the earth, without sufficient cause, an unexplained, and I think the
more one examines it an unexplainable, phe-
nomenon, by any process of what calls itself
science.

But its independence of the world, and of
all the world holds, is boldly assumed and as-
serted, by its deliberate turning about upon

nature and demanding that nature shall answer to it for its character.

I have cited two great names in science, in the act of summoning the world to be judged at the bar of human conscience. Mr. Mill condemns nature as cruel and inhuman. But equally St. Paul, though with a larger as well as wiser and more hopeful thought, long since declared that " the whole creation groans and travails together " and "the creation is made subject to vanity." Mr. Spencer, compelled by the fatal necessities of his narrow materialism, declares nature at every instant to be absolutely beneficent, and every possible act of man to be equally good.

St. Paul sees the evil in nature which any man can see who does not shut his eyes, but sees also the meaning, and is the one rational philosopher of the three, and the one whose philosophy is that of progress, genuine evolution, and therefore hope.

Creation is at the bar of *his* moral judgment as at that of Mr. Mill, full of vanity and inconsequence, full of pain and apparent unreason, and in bondage and corruption. But it waits. The years are moving on. The sons of God are revealing. The light breaks the darkness. The world is imperfect. But it is not mad, nor bad, nor accursed, nor vile. A good world, but capable of being made far better, is St. Paul's judgment. Just as human nature is good but imperfect, and therefore under strain of toil and pain, so the kosmos in which it lives is good but imperfect, laboring under stress and strain for the day of its perfection.

Therefore St. Paul's moral judgment of the nature of things is an echo far down the centuries of the voice from the palm-tree of Deborah. The creature is, notwithstanding all temporary triumphs of evils, all successes of wrong and injustice, but struggling onward to " the glorious liberty." The supreme law is good. The stars in their courses fight against Sisera. The fight is bitter, the battle sore, and sometimes long time doubtful, and many a good knight of God is trampled down, and many a white banner trailed in the dust, but there can be but one end—the unswerving stars, the awful dim powers that are so inscrutable to science, are on the side of right, the kosmos is moral as well as rational, and though right be on the scaffold and wrong be on the throne,

" Yet that scaffold sways the future,
And God stands within the shadow,
Keeping watch upon his own."

And now which of these views best answers
to the facts ?  Which of these decisions is the
most "scientific" in the true sense of that
word ?

First of all we may appeal to the testimony
of mankind, the witness of their universal conviction, that there is an eternal and absolute
right, and that the ordered world is upon its
side, under whatever stress and pain ; and this
conviction is just the clearest and most persistent, where men have learned most about
the world and the action of what people call
nature's laws, and where they are most earnestly endeavoring themselves for the betterment of men.

The savage may stand in terror of nature,
as revengeful, unjust, malignant, or evil in
some of its powers.  We have no such terror.
*We* do not seek to placate a power of which
the more we know the more we know it is
on our side.  Mr. Spencer declares "the power
that lies behind phenomena" inscrutable, Mr.
Matthew Arnold is sure that this inscrutable power "makes for righteousness" at all
events.  That much is as clear to the dainty

English scholar as it was to the wise old
Hebrew seeress.  On that same conviction
we are all acting, we who think or speak or
work for the good of men.

There is no progress possible, no real evolving, if the world be diabolic.  There is none, if
it be indifferent.  If the nature of things be
evil, then destruction and not evolution is the
only hope.  If it be indifferent, why should
men work for the enlightenment or betterment
of men in a kosmos stupid to good or ill?

Our hands and tongues are paralyzed for
any human, reasonable, or beneficent uses.
We are men without good in the present and
utterly without hope in the future.  Swift
sweeping out of being of such a universe,
would be the only thing left to desire,—the
only cry of any prayer.

We must leave unsolved the mystery of the
struggle.  That certainly is inscrutable.  The
origin of evil is an enigma of science.  Of
science, I say, because evil exists—that is a fact
known.  How it exists and why it exists belongs to science, if any fact belongs to it.  But
its beginning is as inscrutable as all beginnings.
Certainly the evolution hypothesis does not explain the fact by denying it or ignoring it.

We find the fact and accept it unexplained, though if we should clear it of our confusions it would be well. Pain, suffering, death even, are not parts of the evil in question. The shallowest of all points of view of the nature or meaning of evil, is that of the Hedonist. Bitterest pain, sorest sorrow, anguish, torment, and death do not touch man's well-being, nor are they his real terrors when he *is* a man and proposes to stay one. As a bright writer puts it : " The pleasant, little, perpetual, intellectual, and scientific tea-party of the evolutionist's paradise is not much loftier than Mohammed's, and would become in time something of a dreary bore."

After all, if we grasped the idea that *the essential evil for a man lies in his not being as much of a man as he ought to be*, we might find the problem simplified even to science.

But taking the fact of the struggle which all men see, I say it is unexplainable by any physical theories, how men come to have universally the judgment as to which side is the right side, and also how they universally decide that nature is on that side and works with them, fights for them, and for it, and that in the long run both they and it will be victorious.

The cruel, sensual, Midianitish power perished. The evil Canaanitish powers one by one were swept away. On the walls of Nineveh and Babylon were written the same judgment and the same condemnation. One by one sure ruin comes upon the strongest and richest of the great unrighteous, greedy, sensual powers. The heavens condemn them. The earth casts them out. The kingdoms of righteousness alone stand, and stand while they stay righteous. The ages have a moral judgment, and pronounce moral sentences, and the sentences are somehow executed. Rome falls; and even Gibbon sees that the causes of the fall are moral. The nature of things has pronounced judgment. Jerusalem perishes because it has opposed the moral law of nature, and the law vindicates itself. So continuous is the experience, that it requires no gift of prophecy to foretell a nation's ruin, and yet the nation may be strong and wise and prudent in all things but righteousness. Philosophic history fails not to attribute national ruin to national wrong.

In the long run and, of course, in an imperfect world, with exceptions that prove the rule, it is with families and individuals as with nations. In the ethical realm there is, as in the natural, a law of the survival of the fittest. Temporary success may postpone, but does not avert, the issue. Fraud, cruelty, selfishness, sensuality, cowardice, lying—do these prosper ? Do the families or the individuals that trust in them stand in this world ? If you can pronounce any thing a law, you can pronounce this a law of nature—that they perish, that the sins of the fathers are visited upon the children, and that nature in due time spews them out. A wise and beneficent law is ever working to exterminate the vile, the cowardly, the bad.

And here, and by no means in Mr. Darwin's theory of the descent of man, do I find explanation of the existence of degraded and decaying races. They are not types of the primitive shape and state of men at all, as far as ascertained facts go to show. They are, historically and by sure paleontological facts, in many cases at least, merely races of degraded men perishing by the working of a righteous law. The American Indian was found living on the ruins of a civilization which had perished, and so rapidly going to destruction by his own vices, that, if a white man had never landed

here, it is doubtful whether there would have
been many more Indians in the country than
there are to-day.    This decaying and degraded
race were specimens of a people on which the
beneficent, eternal law was working ; and it was
rapidly killing, scalping, and burning itself off
the face of the earth.

In many groups of the South Sea Islands
the facts are the same.    The Central American
tribes were living on the ruins of a forgotten
civilization.    It is better to stand by facts as
they are, than to be misled by the romances of
Mr. Cooper about the Indians, or the romance
of Mr. Darwin about primitive man.    The
best  physiologists  tell  us  that  even  " the
Neanderthal man," judging by his skull, had
as good a brain as the average Frenchman ;
and if the Eskimos be survivals of the mythical " Miocene men," they have survived because of many most admirable traits, which,
Captain Parry emphatically thought, might be
well  imitated  by  Europeans.    They  are  far
enough from Mr. Darwin's imaginary ape who
first insisted on dispensing with his tail.

Nay, it is not development of the tooth and
claw of brute force that has caused survival in
this world.    A great law, working steadily,

has been forgotten. Nature has had a moral
quality in her. Even the geological records
hand in their testimony. The ravening mon-
sters of the primal slime are stranded wrecks
upon the shores of the theoretic geologic ages.
Armed and furnished to survive by destruction
of all else, nature has cast them out. She has
ever been working out the man, while ape and
tiger die.

He was no Christian who sang :

> " Gentleness, wisdom, virtue, and endurance,
> These are the seals of that most firm assurance
> That bars the pit over destruction's strength."

The gentle powers, the ordered, sweetly
reasonable, and kindly gifts of humanity, are
the strong gifts in a nation, or in a man. It
would seem as if nature was the enemy, when
it comes to him at least, of mere force.

" God is on the side of the heaviest artillery,"
was the notion of one, than whom no man
blundered worse in his understanding of the
world and nature. Faith in force and destiny,
that was all. And on the sea-washed rock of
St. Helena his faith left him stranded, because,
as Carlyle would say, " the eternal veracities
were against his lie."

A materialistic fatalism which has no place

for morals—which knows no right and no wrong, is working itself into the thought of the time. It will work itself still more deeply as time passes. Its issue, when accepted by any people, can be, if there be any thing sure in experience,—that is in genuine *scientia*—only ruin soon or late. Blind pride and blind trust in mere force have a persistent result.

And this fatalism challenges for itself the name of science, and sets itself out as the one true thing. If it be so, then we must accept the consequences. No matter what the fact be in science, we must face the fact. The consequences must take care of themselves.

But I must decline to call it science, must decline to accept it because it does not explain all the facts nor satisfy most essential conditions. It is not that it is opposed to religion, or needs to be reconciled with religion. It is, that it requires me to believe the unbelievable, and accept the unthinkable, results without causes, ends without purpose.

A creature stamped moral, with the " I ought" uttering itself in him, in some dialect, wherever found; with the sense of duty and right, whatever he may mean by them, sovereign over his nature though he may rebel;

with this overbearing moral conviction of " the
thing he ought," in the best types of the race
in all ages, driving him to endure misery,
hunger, pain, death, binding him in the dungeon, chaining him to the stake, sharpening
the axe for him at the block; with the moral
judgment of the race powerless to imitate him
in its millions, still by its millions uttering
itself in "Well done! this becomes a man";
such a creature comes out, I am asked to
believe, from the blind working of blind matter,
is evolved and descended from mere "stoff"!

Again, this being has the living conviction
that not only ought he to be righteous, but
that whatever claims his reverence and regard
or manly fear should be righteous also; that
his God, if he have a god, must be at least as
good as a good man, that the world in which
he lives must be a world that makes for righteousness—shall not be a brutal nor a devilish
thing. With that persistent instinct he turns
upon the world, as we have seen, and questions it about its morals and its meaning, hesi-
tates not to measure it by his human moral
judgment, and condemn it, if he think it wrong,
with scorn and defiance. And I am asked to
believe that blind force and blind matter

evolved this being, who insists on turning
upon them and judging them both by the
moral law that flames within him ! Force
binds Prometheus to the rock of matter, but
Prometheus defies them both, even with the
vulture at his liver,—defies them, and holds himself a man. The old myth is truer to the fact
than the new science.

So I am driven, as the vast mass of men
have been driven in all ages, and as the highest, best, and wisest have been glad to confess
themselves driven, to hold the kosmos, with all
the difficulties of the case, not only reasonable
but moral. This, at all events : no matter how
inscrutable the power behind phenomena, the
facts assure me that He is righteous and works
out righteousness in its time.

So only can I account for any moral law at
all in man ; that the world was made and is
sustained by a moral power outside man, to
which the moral law inside answers ; that here
there is the objective law to answer to the subjective conviction ; that the " I ought " in man
has an eternal " I ought," which is beyond cir-
cumstance and beyond time ; that the conscience of man postulates a God of righteousness.

So I and my kind, in this blind clash of force and stuff can stand secure. It is no blind clash or brute whirl of iron wheels, but a world rolling daily out into the fairer day—eternal reason working hitherto, and eternal right evolving all things well, crushing as it rolls the bestial and the bad, and wheeling into triumph the manly and the good.

And we can work and we can suffer, we can fight and, if need be, fall. We can be trampled under the iron hoofs of force and triumphant wrong, and still, with sure conviction, turn dying eyes to the eternal watching stars, and hear the cry come down uttering the conviction of saint and sage, of patriot and hero, of the deliverers of men and the shepherds of the people, in the hour when they fought and fell or conquered, "The stars in their courses fight against Sisera."

Part VI. of Herbert Spencer's "Principles of Sociology," after more than three years since the issue of the preceding volume, has been published under the title "Ecclesiastical Institutions" (D. Appleton & Co.). It discusses the origin and development of the religious idea, the rise of a priesthood, with its civil and military functions, and moral influences, and concludes with a religious retrospect and prospect. Mr. Spencer believes that with the transition from theism to agnosticism "all observances implying the thought of propriation may be expected to lapse." But there will still remain a need for qualifying the prosaic form of life with observances "tending to keep alive a consciousness of the relation in which we stand to the Unknown Cause." And in future evolved intelligences this religious feeling will grow deeper and broader. To the man of the future "there will remain the one absolute certainty that he is ever in presence of an Infinite and Eternal Energy, from which all things proceed."

# 1885.

# FOUNDER'S DAY

AT

## Gambier.

# FOUNDERS' DAY.

---

## ORDER OF SERVICE

NOVEMBER 3, 1885,

AS ON

## *THE FESTIVAL OF ALL SAINTS.*

---

*OFFICIATING PERSONS:*

| | |
|---|---|
| THE TE DEUM . | . . . Kenyon College Choir. |
| ANTE-COMMUNION | { Rt. Rev. Dr. Knickerbocker, Bishop of Indiana. |
| THE EPISTLE . | { Rt. Rev. Dr. Whitehead, Bishop of Pittsburgh, |
| THE GOSPEL | { Rt. Rev. Dr. Thompson, Assistant Bishop of Mississippi. |
| THE CREED | The Bishop of Pittsburgh. |
| FOUNDERS' MEMORIAL | { Rt. Rev. Dr. Bedell, Bishop of Ohio. |

DOXOLOGY.
PRAYER FOR THE INSTITUTIONS.
HYMN 232 AT 3D VERSE.

| | |
|---|---|
| THE FIRST LECTURE. | { Rt. Rev. Hugh Miller Thompson, D.D. |

HYMN 494.
OFFERTORY FOR FOUNDERS' SCHOLARSHIP.
MATRICULATION OF THE THEOLOGICAL SEMINARY.
MATRICULATION OF KENYON COLLEGE.
THE HOLY COMMUNION—The Bishops Present.

# FOUNDERS' DAY.

## THE SECOND LECTURE.

### ORDER OF SERVICE

AS FOR THE

MEETING OF THE

## CENTRAL CONVOCATION OF THE DIOCESE.

| | |
|---|---|
| THE LITANY  . | { Rev. Sherlock A. Bronson, D.D., Rector of Grace Church, Mansfield, Ohio. |
| HYMN. | |
| THE SECOND LECTURE  . | { Rt. Rev. Hugh Miller Thompson, D.D., Assistant Bishop of Mississippi. |
| BENEDICTION  . | { Rt. Rev. David Buel Knickerbocker, D.D., Bishop of Indiana. |

# FOUNDERS' DAY AT GAMBIER, 1883.

WE REMEMBER BEFORE GOD this day the Founders of these Institutions : PHILANDER CHASE, the first Bishop of Ohio, *clarum et venerabile nomen*, whose foresight, zeal, unwearied patience, and indomitable energy devised these foundations, and established them temporarily at Worthington, but permanently at Gambier ; he was the Founder of the Theological Seminary, Kenyon College, and of the Grammar School ;—CHARLES PETTIT MCILVAINE, the second Bishop of Ohio, rightly known as the second Founder of these Institutions, whose decision of character and self-devoted labors saved them at two distinct crises of difficulty ; he builded Bexley Hall for the use of the Theological Seminary, Ascension Hall for the use of Kenyon College, Milnor Hall for the use of the Grammar School, and he completed Rosse Chapel on the foundations laid by Bishop Chase.

We remember before God this day pious and generous persons, contributors, whose gifts enabled the Bishops of Ohio to lay those foundations, and who are therefore to be named among the Founders. We make mention only of those who have departed to be with Christ, and now rest in Paradise.

Among the many, we name only a few whose gifts are noticeable because of the influence of their character and position :

HENRY CLAY, whose introduction of Bishop Chase to the ADMIRAL LORD GAMBIER, of England, initiated the movement in 1823 ; the ARCHBISHOP of Canterbury ; the LORD BISHOPS of London, Durham, St. Davids, Chester, Lichfield ; the DEANS of Canterbury and Salisbury ; LORDS Kenyon, Gambier, Bexley, Sir Thomas Acland ; Reverend Edward Bickersteth, Henry Hoare, Marriott, Pratt, WILLIAM WILBERFORCE, Thomas Wiggin, Thomas Bates ; the Dowager COUNTESS OF ROSSE, who aided liberally the Chapel which afterward bore her name ; HANNAH MORE, who also bequeathed a Scholarship which bears her name ; and five hundred and thirty others whose names are recorded in the memorial prepared by the Rev. Dr. Bronson at the order of the Trustees.

We remember before God the liberality of WILLIAM HOGG, from whom this domain was purchased under the advice of Henry B. Curtis and Daniel S. Norton, with the consent of Henry Clay ; the grantor contributing one fourth of its market value.

In 1838, JOHN QUINCY ADAMS, the President of the United States ; Mrs. Sigourney ; Arthur Tappan, who originated the Milnor Professorship ; St. George's Church, New York, which established a Scholarship ; Rev. Drs. Milnor, Tyng, Bedell, Sparrow, Keith, Rev. I.

Morse, Dudley Chase, Albert Barnes, John Trimble, William Jay, Abbott and Amos Lawrence, Peter Stuyvesant, Richard Varick, and nine hundred and ninety others whose names are recorded.

These were the first Founders of these Institutions.

Among those who aided Bishop McIlvaine we mention before God to-day,—in 1832, BISHOP WHITE, Rev. Manton Eastburn and the Ascension Church, the Rev. Dr. Cutler and St. Ann's Church, Brooklyn, the Rev. Drs. Muhlenberg and Wing, Peter A. Jay, James Lennox, Robert Minturn, Henry Codman, Robert Carter, Matthew Clarkson, Charles Hoyt, I. N. Whiting, and four hundred and sixty others whose names are recorded.

And in 1835, in England, Daniel Wilson, Bishop of Calcutta; the Bishops of London, Winchester, Salisbury, and Lichfield; the DUCHESS OF KENT, the Duchess of Gloucester, the Princess Augusta, the Duchess of Beaufort, the Earl of Carnarvon, Rev. Thomas Hartwell Horne, Charles Brydges, John Fox, Jerram, Jowett, Baptist Noel, Dr. Plumtre, Charles Simeon, Henry Thornton, Sir Thomas Baring, Henry Roberts, architect, who gave the plan and working model for Bexley Hall; with four hundred and eighty-three others whose names are recorded.

These are the second Founders of these Institutions.

We mention before God to-day the gifts of Bishop Gadsden, Bishop Johns, Colonel Pendleton, John Kilgour, the Kinneys, Dr. Doddridge, Charles D. Betts, who founded a fund for the purchase of theological books; Rev. C. C. Pinkney, who contributed for fitting up a Laboratory; J. D. Wolfe, who contributed to found the Lorillard and Wolfe Professorships; John Johns, M.D., of Baltimore, who left a valuable legacy to the Institutions; Stewart Brown, William H. Aspinwall, and others who contributed to the building of Ascension Hall; Thomas H. Powers, Lewis S. Ashurst, John Bohlen and sister, and others who founded a Professorship in memory of the late Dr. Bedell of Philadelphia; Mrs. Spencer, Mrs. Lewis, who partly founded a Professorship, Rev. Dr. Brooke; Rev. Messrs. Lounsberry and E. A. Strong, whose efforts brought many valuable contributions to these Institutions; W. W. Corcoran, President Andrews, Rev. Alfred Blake, and nine hundred and forty others who are also to be counted among the Founders of these Institutions.

And last, the Philanthropist, GEORGE PEABODY, the intimate friend of Bishop McIlvaine, who, in token of that friendship founded a Professorship that bears his name.

We mention before God to-day, with reasons that none can better appreciate than this community, which mourns their loss, three of our citizens, recorded among the Founders: Rev. Marcus T. C. Wing, D.D., who, besides being a Professor in the Theological Seminary, was for thirty years financial agent and book-keeper. More than

7,000 acres of our land was sold by him, at fair profit, and under his direction, $100,000 economically expended in buildings for these Institutions; R. S. French, who, with the assistance of friends in Gambier and Mount Vernon, provided the full set of nine bells and the clock, and placed them in the tower, with power to ring the Canterbury chimes : Martinbro White, who was for twenty years Agent and Treasurer of these Institutions, a man of singular probity and purity, whose character and work, whose fidelity to his trust, whose honesty as well as honorable dealing during difficult times when these foundations were being laid, entitle him not only to a place in our grateful recollection, but to a place among the chief Founders of these Institutions.

Among the donors who are living we mention with gratitude WILLIAM E. GLADSTONE, Member of Parliament (at present Prime-Minister), Rev. Canon Carus, and J. Pye Smith ;—of the United States, Rev. Drs. Dyer and Burr, Professor Francis Wharton, A. H. Moss, M. M. Granger, John Gardiner ; Rev. Archibald M. Morrison, who founded the Griswold Professorship ; Peter Neff, Jr., who gave the Telescope and Transit Instrument ; the Rev. Drs. Muenscher and Bronson, and several hundred others whose names are recorded.

The third Bishop of Ohio, with the aid of William H. and John Aspinwall, James M. Brown, Samuel D. Babcock, William B. Astor, and other members of the Ascension Church of New York, builded the Church of the

Holy Spirit for the use of all the Institutions ; through him Mrs. Bowler founded the Professorship which bears her husband's name, R. B. Bowler, who gave a philosophical apparatus, and who, with Larz Anderson, Henry Probasco, William Proctor, and others, founded the McIlvaine Professorship ; Jay Cooke founded the Professorship which bears his father's name ; Frank E. Richmond founded the Hoffman Library Fund ; Stewart Brown builded the tower of the Church, to bear the name of his son, Abbott Brown. By the same Bishop and his wife the Organ was placed in the Church as a memorial of the second Bishop of the Diocese, and the Episcopal chair as a memorial of the great Founder; members of the Church in Philadelphia completed the endowment of the Bedell Professorship, among them chiefly William Welsh, John Bohlen and his sister, and Thomas H. Powers, who also left a Fund in the hands of the Vestry of Christ Church, Germantown, for a perpetual supply of specified books for students in Bexley Hall ; and Robert H. Ives and his wife, who stated that, desiring not to trammel the Trustees, they placed their fund in the Treasury without conditions.

In 1875 the Trustees determined to found a " Trustees' Professorship," which is partially completed.

All these, and seventy others, are also to be counted among the Founders.

We mention with gratitude the successful efforts of the present President of Kenyon College to complete the endowments, and the gifts which have resulted therefrom, namely, from R. B. HAYES, PRESIDENT OF THE UNITED STATES, Peter Hadyen, Dr. I. T. Hobbs, Rev. William Horton, Thomas McCulloch, Samuel L. Mather, William J. Boardman, A. C. Armstrong, H. P. Baldwin ; from John W. Andrews a donation in lands for the founding of Scholarships in memory of his son ; from Mrs. Alfred Blake donations for the purpose of founding a Scholarship to bear her husband's name ; from Columbus Delano the Hall which bears his name ; from Mrs. Ezra Bliss a Library Building, which bears the name of " Hubbard Hall," in memory of her brother; and from Henry B. Curtis Scholarships which from generation to generation will foster sound learning. These also, with thirty others, the latest givers to our Institutions, are to be counted among the Founders.

*The congregation rising.*

For all these generous gifts of the living, and for the memory of the dead who were the FOUNDERS of these Institutions, we give hearty thanks to God this day ; ascribing the praise of their benefactions to His almighty grace, and the glory of His most holy Name, who is the God of our fathers and our God, the Father, the Son, and the Holy Ghost, ONE ADORABLE TRINITY for ever and ever. Amen.

### PRAYER FOR THE INSTITUTIONS.

O God the Holy Ghost, fountain of all wisdom, source of all grace, be present always, we beseech Thee, with these Institutions to direct and bless.  Established in the faith of the Gospel, endowed for the service of divine truth, may they ever rest under Thy gracious benediction. We pray Thee to use them for the glory of Christ in His Church, and to make them pure fountains of heavenly knowledge, holy principles, and godly learning.  We beseech Thee to give to those who teach in them wisdom and patience, discreetness and zeal for God ; and to those who are taught, aptness to learn, docility, submission without servility, and manly gentleness.  O Holy Spirit, make these Thy servants studious, truthful, pure, obedient to all who are in authority, and temperate in all things ; so that, by Thy grace, the same mind may be in them which was in Christ Jesus our Lord, and their character be formed in his holy likeness.  Prosper Thou, O Lord, the work of our hands upon us !  Give to Thy people a liberal heart toward these Institutions.  May the memory of those whose gifts have enriched us be ever precious in our sight, as it is blessed of God !  And may the good name of these Institutions be handed down from generation to generation for the comfort of Thy Church, and the glory of Thy Majesty, Who art, with the Father and the Son, the One God whom we adore for ever and ever. Amen.

## THE PRAYER OF LORD BACON.

### ADAPTED FOR STUDENTS.

To God the Father, God the Word, and God the Holy Spirit, we pour forth most humble and hearty supplications; that He, remembering the infirmities of our minds, the limits of our knowledge, and the pilgrimage of this our life, in which we wear out days few and evil, would please to open to us new refreshments out of the fountain of His goodness and wisdom. This also we humbly and earnestly beg, that human things may not prejudice such as are divine; neither that from the unlocking of the gates of sense, and the kindling of a greater natural light, any thing of incredulity or intellectual night may arise in our minds toward divine mysteries. But rather that by the cleansing of them through the study of truth, and the purging them from fancy and vanities by the entrance of wisdom, yet subject and perfectly given up to the Divine oracles, there may be given unto our faith the things that are faith's; through Him whom truly to know is everlasting life; and to whom, with Thee O Father, and Thee enlightening Spirit, we ascribe glory and praise world without end. Amen.

www.ingramcontent.com/pod-product-compliance
Lightning Source LLC
Chambersburg PA
CBHW021413090426
42742CB00009B/1122